LAST SEEN

THE FELIX POLLAK PRIZE IN POETRY

LAST
SEEN

Jacqueline Jones LaMon

THE UNIVERSITY OF WISCONSIN PRESS

The University of Wisconsin Press
1930 Monroe Street, 3rd Floor
Madison, Wisconsin 53711-2059
uwpress.wisc.edu

3 Henrietta Street
London WC2E 8LU, England
eurospanbookstore.com

5   4   3   2   1

Printed in the United States of America

Library of Congress Cataloging-in-Publication Data
   LaMon, Jacqueline Jones.
   Last seen / Jacqueline Jones LaMon.
      p.   cm. — (The Felix Pollak prize in poetry)
   ISBN 978-0-299-28294-3 (pbk.: alk. paper) — ISBN 978-0-299-28293-6 (e-book)
   1. Missing children—United States—Poetry. 2. African American children—Poetry.
   I. Title. II. Series: Felix Pollak prize in poetry (Series)
   PS3612.A547L37   2011
   811'.6—dc22   2010038896

For all of us who have been missing.
For all of us who have been lost.

These are not natural silences . . .
—Tillie Olsen

CONTENTS

Acknowledgments   ix

POLYGRAPH: THE CONTROL QUESTIONS
Who are you and whom do you love?   3
Where did you come from / how did you arrive?   4
How will you begin?   5
How will you live now?   6
What is the shape of your body?   7
Who is responsible for the suffering of your mother?   8

THE ELSEWHERE CHRONICLES
Preface   11
Mrs. Minor Gives Directions to Strangers   12
Two Waffles and a Tall Glass of Milk   13
The Clairvoyant Channels Clea Hall   14
Florida Keys Unidentified   15
Ten Items or Less   16
The Age-Progression Artist Pencils Thicker Lashes   17
A Suspect Mother Answers during Polygraph   18
"Let Me Run Upstairs and Get My Purse . . ."   19
Back Roads   20
How the Bryant Boy Will Know   21
The Facial Reconstructionist Has Cocktails with the Girls   22
Inheritance   23
Loony 'Toons   24
Last Seen   25
The Network News Director Addresses His Process of Selection   26
For My Husband, Who Took Our Daughter to the Park So I Could Get
    Some Rest, Then Fell Asleep and Awakened to an Empty Stroller   27

BOY MET GIRL

At the Carnival, Near Prospect Park 31
Through a Mutual Friend 32
At Lance and Carol's Wedding 33
In July, at Nathan's Clam Bar 34
On the Tennis Courts 35
At B. Altman's Department Store 36
On the Subway 37
At Rockaway Beach, in Late June 38
At Claire's Father's Funeral 39

THE SAN FRANCISCO SONNETS

The Taker Returns from a Ten-Minute Break 43
San Francisco Bridge Suicide Jumper Considers Relativity 44
The Missing Girl's Sister 45
Prom King Goes Stag His Senior Year 46
The Junior Detective's Wife Speaks Out on the Day of Their Divorce 47
The Missing Girl's Mother 48
Priest Refuses Comment on Accident Driver's Acquittal 49
Olympic Hopeful Assesses Her Victory 50
The Missing Girl's Cousin 51
The Present Song of Seagulls on the San Francisco Bay 52
The Missing Girl's Boyfriend 53
The Teacher Prepares the Crisis Counseling Team 54
Couple Tours Alcatraz on Their Silver Anniversary 55
The Missing Girl's Father 56

POLYGRAPH: THE GUILTY KNOWLEDGE TEST

• • • 59
What do you remember about the earth? 60
What are the consequences of silence? 61
Tell me what you know about dismemberment 62
Describe a morning you woke without fear 63
And what would you say if you could? 64
How will you / have you prepare(d) for your death? 66

Note 67

ACKNOWLEDGMENTS

I wish to thank Adelphi University, the Cave Canem Foundation, Inc., Indiana University Bloomington, the Key West Literary Seminars, and the Virginia Center for the Creative Arts for their most generous support during the creation of this work.

For recommendations, advice, and literary reflection during the five years of gestation, I especially thank A. Van Jordan, Judith Baumel, Martha Collins, Stacy Leigh, Kermit Frazier, Linda Susan Jackson, Dr. Nzadi Keita, Dr. Duriel Harris, Kevin Young, Maura Stanton, Catherine Bowman, Sharon Dolin, Michael S. Harper, Terrance Hayes, Tayari Jones, Dr. Bettina Judd, and my literary agent, Sara Camilli.

I offer a very special thank you to Dana, Winter, Linnea, Dana C., and Anton for affording me the time and space to take this journey into Elsewhere.

Grateful acknowledgement is made to the editors of the following publications in which these poems appear, sometimes in different versions:

Bellevue Literary Review: "Describe a morning you woke without fear"
Crab Orchard Review: "How the Bryant Boy Will Know"
Mythium: "And what would you say if you could?"
Ninth Letter: "The Age-Progression Artist Pencils Thicker Lashes,"
    "For My Husband: Who Took Our Daughter to the Park So I Could Get
    Some Rest, Then Fell Asleep and Awakened to an Empty Stroller"
Quercus Review: "The Facial Reconstructionist Has Cocktails with the Girls"
RATTLE: "Who are you and whom do you love?"

Polygraph: The Control Questions

Who are you and whom do you love?

The woman you were when you left them. The silhouette
sorting through your garbage, in search of aluminum
cans and credit cards. The man who jumped
in front of your car and the man who thought
he had pushed him. The jealous husband. Clarence Thomas's
first wife. The minister who built harpsichords
and molested you, again and again. The mother who cannot
taste her milk. Your grandmother's image of herself.
Sammy Davis Jr. Your children. The children you knew
would die as sacrifice. The man who wears headphones
and operates the ride. The child running into the fire,
for protection. The reprieved. The stoic who embraces
his weakness. The woman you swear you have become.

Where did you come from / how did you arrive?

They threw a costume party and dressed up as themselves.
Doctors becoming vampires stuck on the quantity of days,
their nurses arriving as witches, independent and oblique,
the managers, stoic as morticians on the cemetery's hill.

The doctors, just like vampires stuck on the quantity of days,
watch the dentists go from chair to chair, sharing sordid jokes
with the managers, stoic as morticians on the cemetery's hill.
They all wait for the bathroom near your parents' kitchen door.

Your father, the dentist, going from chair to chair, shares sordid jokes
about not knowing the resident patients from the certified staff.
They laugh and wait for the bathroom near your parents' kitchen door,
jack-o'-lanterns casting shadows on the walls of every room.

No one knows the resident patients from the certified staff,
the dead portraying the living, the living dolled up as the dead.
Jack-o'-lanterns cast shadows on the walls of every room,
as your mother knocks, in threes, on the locked bathroom door.

The dead portray the living, the living dolled up as the dead.
The custodian, now a mummy, produces a ring of skeleton keys
while your mother knocks, in threes, on the locked bathroom door—your mother,
so pregnant, calling the name of your father's absent colleague.

The custodian, now a mummy, produces a ring of skeleton keys
and finds the one that fits inside the bathroom doorknob lock.
So pregnant, and calling the name of your father's absent colleague,
your mother touches the dead one—slumped on the floor, in his costume.

Who finds the one that fits inside the bathroom doorknob lock?
You are born the next day, calling saints and dodging spirits.
Your mother never speaks of him—slumped silhouette, in his costume.
Your parents threw a costume party and dressed up as themselves.

How will you begin?

After they find their bodies on the shoulder
of Route 80, all you can dream about is the yellow
tarp wrapped around their bloodless bodies,
the rumors, the sirens, the strobes.

These were your neighbors—Carol, the designer
who draped and wrote poems, who favored gold
brocade and plush velvets, who exchanged her first
coat for your last five dollars, because *an artist*

never truly gives her work away. And Howard,
her husband, the painter, twenty years her senior
and that many inches taller, who waved at you
each morning and asked what you wanted

to learn from this life. And if they are not here
and the blood is not there, what do you do
when the coat no longer fits and is not
in your new hall closet? You sing

into the street from the windows you left open.
You sing until the people gather, pausing in front
of that infamous apartment, looking all around
themselves, to wonder who and what they hear.

How will you live now?

The night ignites this evil. You pick up the phone
and call the rich, pretty girl who considers you
slightly too fringed. You hear the dial tone, swirl
the rotary, then notice the undersides of things,
the dirt beneath the window sill, the nonskid reverse
of your yellow shag rug.

You tell her the lie—the boy was shot, killed,
and you are sorry but you must go. You hang up
but not before you hear the wails of her sister
in the background, the footsteps of their mother
running to catch them in their fall.

[Insert here a section of justification—because you were
green, both envious and young. Because you were acting
on some now-imagined dare, some wound that festered
in hindsight, a ramification of race discrimination or class.]

The executioner's pain is only measurable
from a comfortable distance. No one talks to you
save the boy and his mother and they are both alive,
relieved but disappointed.

How many times can you kill and expect to witness resurrection?

There are gunshots all around you every night.
Your daughters carry textbooks through war zones
and your sons have open battle scars. You live and pray
for redemption. You turn off all your telephones at night.

What is the shape of your body?

When you do your dance in the dark,
the mirrors say you are turbulence
and agony, the conical form of deep
green twister, a violent agate storm.
How can a tangible ever be wrong?
You question the images before you,
your mind's eye adrift, your reflection
performing without your consent. See it
for yourself—your arms beveled about
your seated concave torso, your legs bent,
one before you, one behind. You contract,
hold this weighty pose of pain for years.

Who is responsible for the suffering of your mother?

You never believe it can happen, but it does every day—
dawn on DeKalb is without breath or even a clearing
of throats. A parked truck. An empty bus stop. Only
a rapid set of footsteps in a rush for what's beyond. The roses
beneath your bedroom window scent your last true dream.
This is not the same land present the night before,
when Two Steps Down hosted a woman and her bass—
the sane land it will be once the church people stand
outside Mike's, delighted to slide into the narrow booth in the back.
You sit on your breezeway with your Chock full o'Nuts, grateful
for the lush hanging fern above your head, the wrought iron and the glass . . .

The Elsewhere Chronicles

I was waiting for my children. We were late for something important, for my son's performance at the high school or my daughter's track meet. I paced and caught myself, walked over to the table strewn with mail: too many bills, a circular or two, a magazine. I picked up the magazine and flipped through the pages, hoping to hear my son bounding down the stairs, two at a time, hoping to hear my daughter zipping her sweatshirt and humming.

There were photographs, pages of them. I thought they were age-progression renderings of girls, African American girls. Girls with magnified eyes that remembered violence coming toward them, their terror present even in the drawings. We couldn't linger; my son and daughter reminded me that it really was time for us to go. My children ran without me to our car, unlocked at the curb. I tossed aside the magazine and followed them.

That night, I visited the online site for the National Center for Missing and Exploited Children for the first time, hoping to see more about these girls and their stories. To begin, I conducted a more general search: African Americans, males and females, all categories of circumstances, the past fifty years. Hundreds of faces appeared on my computer screen.

Each face has a name. *Name me.* Each name has a poster. *Look at me.* Each poster states the child's last recorded appearance and, perhaps, what that child was wearing. *Find me.* I had never heard of any of these children, but I know they own a collective voice I strain to hear. What we hear in our daily lives is the voice of their absence. This silence is the source of these poems.

Mrs. Minor Gives Directions to Strangers

Turn LEFT at the second light
Follow the road until the three-way fork
Make a slight no that cannot be RIGHT
Think about all that is LEFT
His eyes, his crib, his socks are STRAIGHT AHEAD
RIGHT, past dark. RIGHT, past darkness.

No. Let me start again.

STOP at the light years from now you will never
Know this TURN AROUND but you keep moving
On, GO ON until you reach the corner of anywhere
Now, navigate the CIRCLE, bearing to his memory
Keep going, until you until you reach don't stop
until you don't stop until you reach the corner
of some dank street and rundown avenue until nothing
is LEFT until keep going don't stop until you
HERE, was just here and you see him don't oh please
wait nothing is reach don't stop until you find my boy.

Two Waffles and a Tall Glass of Milk

Anyways, she mumbled, fumed. He'd wandered, thought
back to the last thing he could have asked. He
could have asked about her folks, what she
did to earn her keep, but when could he have found that
entrance? He rubbed stubble, played with his waffle, his
fork, thought about his mother. How she would
get sometimes, full of spirits on a blue plaid
hot summer's night, beat his father to know not one
in the name of cockeyed justice. Eye for a roaming eye
justice. And she would stop when the sun came up,
kind of tired, almost spent. To think they called that
love. He looked at this fresh one—twelve, thirteen at
most, ready and ripe. She hadn't yet learned how to say
no to a man. She sipped. Outside, a single pump long
overdue for refill, a teasing oasis for near gasless
passing cars, afternoons apart. He wanted this one
quiet, willed it. Nothing to remind him of weather vanes,
regrets, the man he'd never be. Something tugged inside.
Some song, low moan beneath the kitchen, where Cook
took his runaways on thunderous, closed-in nights.
"Until You Come Back to Me," or so he thought, his mind
veering from one of her bare shoulders to the other.
What a sporting man won't do to gain traction, turn
xenophobe or embracer on a dime. *You know*, he lied,
you could *live with me.* Cook howled, turned to oldies on the
Zenith, turned up the volume crazy high, wiry static and all.

The Clairvoyant Channels Clea Hall

Someone is making his or her way toward me,
no one yet near, no one I know. I've had it

with these clandestine cops, slick ones
who need their info clean, without a trail

behind them. I know they'll swear they had
no help; they know I'll keep their secret. I will tell

my dreams about Miss Hall, my visions clearly Clea—
the files, the noise, the doctor's call, her mother's

dreamless sleeping. I'll tell them how the girl
they seek walked past the sure of twilight,

lost bearings in a winding maze of metal halls
and basements. I dreamt there was this pink balloon—

its ribbon chokes the family tree,
the father left there, dying. Two men

are nearing my back door, through sheets
of horizontal rain, the tremble of my teacup.

Florida Keys Unidentified

DNA analysis: A female.
   Of biracial—no, unknown
      descent. Sixteen, maybe.

Or twenty-five. A past of piercings.
   There is a tattoo of *Love*,
      the answered question, blazed.

And a cross between her fingers,
   with pigment sun now faded,
      almost—but not quite—gone.

Ten Items or Less

JenJen wasn't giving up
a sip of her soda, not even
a taste, not even to her sister.
Too bad: she waited all day
for the syrup and fizz,
their father dropping them
off in a humid heat hurry,
then hightailing himself
on to work. *Watch out for her*
he'd said, so JenJen watched
the girl suck her teeth, twist
a loose braid, settle into her hip
like a woman long since grown
and able. She watched her whine
and stomp her feet, then try
to snatch the straw away, saw
her crumbled face when Jen
began to laugh. *I have money,
too, you know,* Jasmine said,
then turned into the store,
became the aisles of cereals
and chocolate bars with nuts,
the wobbly, metal grocery carts,
the fashion magazines. She was
last seen here: thirsty and ruffling
her pockets, for change. Summer,
1962. An eight-year-old black girl
in pink pants and flip flops,
who never talked to strangers,
a scar above one eye.

The Age-Progression Artist Pencils
Thicker Lashes

Maybe I overstep, to paint her smile on this way, toothy
and broad curved, the most mindless stare. At twenty-seven,

she would think every day what it means to be taken,
to be lost and in a man's arms, a squirm away from herself,

static, separated. I have to choose so much: to press out
her hair, divide it or gather, cut it off with a chop

because she might have dyed it red-orange, hate the truth
of her whole self by now. Beyond my work window, a mother yells

at her youngest, walks three steps away. He will get no new toy,
no hot chocolate, no whipped cream. His face upturned and deepened,

he does not cry, will not let her be the victor. I test my recall—
hooded navy jacket, yellow plastic boots, crumpled paper bag,

threadbare argyle mittens. He watches her leave, looks away
from the earth, drags his left foot to leave his mark in the snow.

A Suspect Mother Answers during Polygraph

I will tell you the truth
I did not sell my son
I will tell you everything I know

    I took things that didn't belong to me and made them mine
    I never lied to a raised voice in uniform
    Of course I kept his clothes

      I once held a bird, and crushed it, by mistake
      I was never stopped for driving drunk
      You do not scare me

        I have two other children, still with me
        I am active in the PTA
        I want to move away, but why

          I always speak the truth
          When a man shakes my shoulders, I ask for forgiveness
          My favorite word is suicide

          When the doorbell rings, I clench my fists
          I know I can breathe underwater
          You need to ask his father

"Let Me Run Upstairs and Get My Purse . . ."

For two months straight, all he did was smile.
Gurgle and rock, his hands clutched into
mini-muffin fists, in wave above his head.
And that hair: mirror enough to reflect a face,
the purest intention, the tiniest thought.

My husband said he ought to be
made famous in a sleek kid magazine, splashed
on a page selling diapers or hope.
Folks said all you need is one fine picture,
one clear eye to see his soul, still

breath filled with next. And on that morning,
when the sun was high and the breeze
was free, my world became glassy, a tumbleweed
of maybe—shiny lies, jagged moves.
Out of nowhere comes this gust,

collar down and handsome, my child perfect
for his portrait special, talking truth I thought I knew:
how my son would make the world happy just taking
in air, how every household would soon know
his face, recite his full name, seek him out like a star.

Back Roads

In and out of tree-lined counties
they swerve and sway to gospel swell
a soprano, a contralto, the intermittent coo

Her baby's in the new car seat
Her baby's in the big-girl chair
Her baby's facing forward now
Her baby sings a Jesus song

Little Miss Lady of Mary Janes and lace
Princess of crinoline, frothy chiffon
Kissing cheeks buffed with Vaseline, honey

Who named this ride eternity?

There's a skip, a skip in this record *Pull Over*
A frozen frame that never fades to black   *Get Out*
A cotton-ripe road that curves invisible, night blind.

How the Bryant Boy Will Know

Their name for you tastes bitter and uncooked.
Do not listen when they say you were adopted.

Hear your given, gnaw upon this gristle.
You are someone's missing boy.

Your father named you
Jeremiah.

Your mother was slaughtered,
set on fire for her newborn.

These people do not spring from you.
Your parents laughed together, married

and sucked marrow. Your sickle cell
was not a fluke, disease come up out

of nowhere. You have two pretty sisters, fourteen
distant cousins. There were three straight generations

of fine, hot-tempered men. Your father never
lost a fight, or slept a dreamless night.

When you crave tender meat, they say they want their money back.
Do not laugh. Find the cash. Follow fresher air.

The Facial Reconstructionist
Has Cocktails with the Girls

I've always had this thing for clay, to cup
my hands around a sphere, allow my fingers'

strength to grope toward definition. I know
there is an art to this, despite the grayness

of my walls. When the cranial remains lie
in state before me, I play *The Lark Ascending,*

let my mind know dawn and flight. Vaughan
Williams and I mold the timing of rise, the hover

preceding the soar. After work, my girlfriends ask
no questions of me. They stare at my hands,

inspect my cuticles for hangnails and fingernails
unkempt, survey the end of the bread that I touch.

They don't ask how I can wade my way through gore,
question unclaimed bones, mold parentheses around

a flesh I'll never know. This victim was a man-child.
I contemplate tissue thickness near his nasal spine,

the skin shade I will choose, the social construction
of race. I have another Cosmo. I think about his eyes.

Inheritance

You believe you are certain
of your lineage. You think
you are balding in the same pattern
as your brother, your uncle.
You pull up weeds at night.
You and your sisters are sensitive
to cold, shiver in even the summer's
rising heat. Your neighbor shivers, too,
tells you to eat more red meat,
to insulate your attic, your shared
thin walls. You scratch until you bleed.
Your fingernails mirror those
of your mother, sport moons
like sunsets over meadows.
You magnify ants to a crisp,
gaze as they panic and curl.
When you cough, your whole house
coughs—your doctor calls it allergies,
your family's guttural response
to the presence of foreign matter.
You learn to tie knots, clean live fish.
Your confidence is a simple matter
of DNA—a strand of hair, a swab
of your inner cheek—congenital
mysteries solved. You drink and drive,
you pass bad checks, convulse
and bite your tongue. You blame
these things on your mother's side.
You never knew your father.
You kill a mouse. You douse a cat.
You smother a man before dinner.

Loony 'Toons

That's all, folks!
—Porky Pig

One day she will come home and her fingers
will reach to turn the knob on a door long
demolished, the neighborhood imploded
years before, like unconfessed guilt, the sin
still there, now sheer but impenetrable.
And logic, we think, says it is easy
to traverse an unobstructed entry,
a place without threshold, shutters, or locks
but then the bruise of attempt remains: truth,
a cartooned reality, sordid joke
of inversion. To return: To claw
through the darkness at every scene's close,
to find other ending, the old porch swing.

Last Seen

at home
near a grocery store four miles east of Woodville on Highway 24
at ten a.m., riding a red bicycle
at home at approximately five p.m. on June 21, 1989
at the Broad Acres Swap Meet
playing video games in his home during the early morning hours of March 30, 1997
on January 21, 2005—may still be in the local area—Tia Anderson: call somebody
walking home from school
walking home from school together
on April 27, 1973, when she left home to go to school
at home
at age twelve, when she was nine months pregnant
at a supermarket in Staten Island, New York
at the New Frontier Lanes Bowling Alley in Tacoma, Washington
outside of her home on February 25
playing in the hallway outside of her apartment
playing in his front yard
playing in her back yard
at home
sitting on her front porch, in a stroller
at home, with a family friend watching
playing tag
leaving a friend's house on New Year's Eve, 1981
at home
getting off of the school bus, near the home of a friend
in a park located on 114th Street and Lenox Avenue
shopping at the Winston-Salem Rayless Department Store on June 13, 1970
getting into a red convertible
on March 24, when she left to go to a nearby store
playing outside with the neighborhood children
down the block from her house, running after an ice-cream truck

The Network News Director Addresses
His Process of Selection

I said I could be ruthless. I said I could
choose between *A* and *B*, select the bigger story
to reflect the greater good. Still, all the staff
waits for me to blackwash breaking news,
to pick out those stories to marquee my race.

The drill's nothing new. I gathered 'Nam footage,
covered hits in Iran, too; I can skew with the best,
see the green prize through gauze. My restricted
carte blanche: to report the planet beyond
myself, to find the blond and rosy. Paint safe

the resort where the sponsor flies, silence bleak
news on lost coeds—one was mangled by locals,
they say. I work within a burlap bag. I am
ripping holes for air. Look to the left, near
the bottom: we are running a crawl on your boy.

For My Husband, Who Took Our Daughter to the Park So I Could Get Some Rest, Then Fell Asleep and Awakened to an Empty Stroller

I know when you dream of her.
You hit at the air, wake up bruised.

Round one: you search for a person,
get sideswiped by soft and rusted metal.

Round two: they will not let you
in the ring. The entrance is gone.

Did you hear her? You thought
you heard her. Quick: where is she?

You awaken in layers: the dream of you
in dream, the underside of sleep.

Round four: you could have found her
in round three, but where were you?

You dream I am inside your dream,
letting you sleep   wake up   sleep   wake up.

BOY MET GIRL

In Memory
of
Julie and Freddy

who never divulged
how they met

At The Carnival, Near Prospect Park

Any moment it would pour; the sky just above,
beyond this field and drooping. I'd wait each year for
carnival, for silly, stuffed animals won by boyfriends
decidedly handsome and lank. I had choices
every year: the fellows called me Lena or "she most
fair," and meant it every time. I knew I looked
good, and Maybelline was my best friend—rouge
high on my cheekbones, liner dark on deep-set eyes,
innocence a hindrance long ago discarded. I was
just one playful woman seeking one gorgeous boy:
kind to his mother but rightly raucous at times,
lustrous on the Ferris wheel, his arm primed to drape
my seat back. All my friends were going steady,
no one single in our crowd then, just me. I'd go
on rides alone this time, buy my own frozen custard,
play to win those small, fluffy prizes at the arcade, sans
quarterback or forward. And I'll admit it was fun:
running from attraction to attracted when I
saw his sweet face. *Excuse me, Miss Pretty Lady?*
Think you'd go with me once through the Tunnel of Love?
Underneath his bravado was a shelter, a threadbare quilt,
vanilla-laced banter and cinnamon sticks. *Well,*
why not? I shrugged, my crinolines rustling like
xylophone highs, his grey felt fedora tipping my way.
You should never ride alone, he blushed. Then the rain fell with
zest, the night all saltwater taffy swirled with the fragrance of hay.

Through a Mutual Friend

Audrey had been my good friend, *had been*
being the operative words. Friends since
childhood, our mothers insistent on weekly
dance lessons for us, ballet and ballroom
equally as important. Everyone thought us
fastened at the hip, twins from stage gawky to
glamorous, the two of us ruling Lane
High together, queen and queen alike.
I never saw it coming. Audrey uncaring,
just leaving me out of the loop of this new crowd,
kicking me to the curb. Well, you know, I
let her have it, in my own sneaky way,
more as a warning than anything else. *He's hers?* He
noticed my stockings first—smooth silk and seamed.
Obedient to beauty—these stockings and men. Her hand
pulled him away from my steady gaze of quiet
questions: *Why are you with her? Give me just one good
reason* . . . Any man knows a cleavage is
stealthy; it calls him back with a whispering
tug. I haven't seen Audrey in thirty-two
upstanding years. Our mothers died softly after
valiant lives. Her eventual husband took a mistress,
walked away from their home, from everything he knew.
X-rated movies are her new favorite thing. All these
years. Yes, the two of us were once like twins,
zappy, twirling like angels throughout our schoolgirl days.

At Lance and Carol's Wedding

Abortion was not a word spoken
by our crowd. And so, when
cornered, or rather, *informed* of this
dilemma, their wedding plans
ensued. I knew that Lance would marry, his
family sweet, upright, and rich—no
girl worth her salt would refuse. I
had to wear pink chiffon, the maid of honor
in rose. Then in walked those groomsmen,
just two, but what a pair. The dark, intellectual
kind, bow tie and cummerbund drenched. We
looked at each other all through the vows,
my smile at the shorter one, discreet and subdued.
No one there knew. When the service was
over, the band took the stand. We *Lindy Hopped*,
practiced our *Madison*—two up, two back—
quite the couple to watch on the dance floor.
Right away, I knew he was the one. We
set our sights on the garden out back,
took our time beneath the arbor, the black
umbrella of the night. He sang "Misty," his
voice an utter scratching post, but still my serenade.
We shared our life's passions: his study of dental
X-rays, amalgams, root canals—and mine,
young children jailed into poverty. He picked up a
zinnia and kissed it. I took it and kissed it once, too.

In July, at Nathan's Clam Bar

Another day of choking humidity.
Brooklyn held in moisture like a sponge,
cheeks crying makeup everywhere. I
didn't want to stay indoors; this
excruciating heat had me dripping like
faucets, my radar attuned to
get some true relief. I'd been to Horn &
Hardart's, roamed the promenade. Yes,
ice cream called my name from Howard
Johnson's—the peppermint loudest of all.
Kegs of frosty beer with Xavier later on, those
lines of mugs waiting at O'Shaunessy's at six.
My escape was Coney Island: train ride for a tasty
nosh—a mustard knish, littleneck clams
on the half shell, frogs' legs, then a pint of
Pabst to wash the whole thing down,
quench my thirst. I felt him come behind me,
request Tabasco from my left. *Done with the hot
sauce?* And I just nodded yes. I watched him
take it, then stand by the counter, balance it all.
Understand now—he ate cherrystones, the huge
variety, and in a single slurp. I took out a cigarette,
waited, rummaged through my purse for a light.
Xavier would end up missing me that day, our
young love ablaze with the stroke of his match, his
zaniness quite charming, a bit off and a little absurd.

On the Tennis Courts

Actually, I didn't like him all that much at first. That
boy thought he was God's gift to pretty girls,
cajoling all us ladies. I had my college-level work to
do, no time for all that nonsense. So many girls so
eager to eyelash bat and swing their skirts. I was his
fascination. And one day on the tennis courts, he
gave us all his number. The nerve, you know? I
had no intention of calling up that Harlem boy, no
interest in wearing his pin or his letterman's
jacket, and gave it not one thought. Still, he had a
knack for making me laugh, despite my reticence.
Love grows from laughter in the easiness of
morning, and he'd caught me hitting balls alone,
no one else there to entertain, no one there but us.
Oblivious to my common sense, I listened to him
purr my name, unleash my better backhand. He turned
quiet when alone with me, like I was his,
resounding. I told myself it was all a sham, my killer
serve would fade away before the coming summer.
That spring, he coached me into my best shape,
unbridling my bristle, barely pleasant to the many girls
vying for his attention. Then clay and grass became my
world, my paradise, my wanting. My treasured trips to
Xanadu were subway rides to Brooklyn, holding hands my
yearning. We'd get off at the library, picnic at Prospect Park
Zoo, talk about our families, the way to serve and volley.

At B. Altman's Department Store

Altman's was crowded so that afternoon, full
because of Mother's Day, with extra
clerks on shift. I wanted to buy her something
dainty—a silk scarf with hand painting,
embroidered handkerchiefs. My mother loved her
fashions, and dressed high for every major
gala or market trip alike. She loved her silver
hairbrush, her mirrored perfume trays.
I imagined her as a young girl, laughing at some
joke, her hair tossed back and wavy, her intuition
keen. She would always wear a pillbox hat, veil
lowered on her eyes. I took the elevator up,
meandering through and gazing, fingering the
nap of a fluid velvet burnout shawl, the fringe
opalescent near my skin. He walked up to me,
perplexed. *You seem to know about these things, the
quality, I mean* . . . And the moment seemed so
radiant—our shopping in B. Altman's, the elegance of
shawls. His eyes were warm and hazel, with flecks of
tarnished bronze. We went to the upstairs cafe
underneath a white-domed skylight, a crystal
vase of baby's breath with rosebuds on each table, where
waitresses glided by with chignons and subtle smiles.
Xylophones tinkled a Cole Porter tune. The both of us
yearned for a little more time, another glass of
zinfandel, a few more plates for grazing.

On the Subway

Abandoned by the rest of the guys, all
buddies from the neighborhood, I took
change from my bureau and caught the
D train downtown. I'd been at my mother's.
Each Sunday her dinners of put-on-weight
food—fried chicken, corn pudding, mixed
greens—would call, her door always opened,
her food always there. Pitchers of peach tea,
iced and sweet beyond belief. I swear I wanted
just one more thigh, just one more bite of that
kale, but we'd said we'd meet out in Brooklyn,
leave our imprint on their courts. I boarded
my train, took a seat parallel to the door
next to a man who talked in his sleep, cried
out for Mommy while everyone laughed. Now,
pretty women I know, but when I saw her cool
quiet, when I saw her slow walk, I stood to her
royalty. *Here, take* my *seat,* I said, even though
seats were empty all around. She smiled, said
Thank you, smoothing the pleats of her skirt
underneath her as she sat. It's funny how the guys
vanish when a woman walks into your life. She
wrote in a notebook and tore out the page. *Any*
x-cuse will do . . . , it read, and so I asked, *So Miss, do*
you mind if I sit next to you? She laughed with a
zest I never had known, the fellas to miss me that day.

At Rockaway Beach, in Late June

Ask anybody—I was a fish out of water when not at the
beach. I was one of those girls who couldn't wait to
caravan across the bridge, swimsuit beneath my eyelet
dress, my hair tied back in a bow. I'd discard all
etiquette, disrobe in front of any guy. This was the beach,
for goodness' sake. This was the way it was. You
grab a friend and pick a spot, the closest to the shore.
Happened that day, we were a group of sullen girls
interested in nothing more than sun, our sandwiches, our
juice. I was out of sorts, I know. My friends were being
kind to me, but I was there for soothing surf. Toppled
love can leave you bent, and I needed to be calmed, a
moment to myself. My guy had thrown me for a loop,
needing space or some gal with housework on her mind.
Other people set up blankets near ours. A father
played catch with his son in wet sand until he turned up
queasy. Two women passed the baby oil, faces
redder than tomatoes. And then this group of guys
sat down, spread three blankets in a row.
They brought a keg of beer with them, some chicken,
ugly plates and such, and several bags of chips. From our
vantage point, the fellas seemed to be alone, seemed to
want our company. For goodness' sake—our chromosome
X could be our excuse, and we could be frail and in need.
Young, jilted, impetuous—I asked help to open a jar,
zigzagging my way through their blankets, finding a better shore.

At Claire's Father's Funeral

Ashes to ashes . . . Only at times like this do we think what we will
become, how we will return to the earth and be remade.
Claire thought of none of this, her hands clenched, eyes closed,
drenched with rain from the uncovered uphill climb. She'd hated
Eddie, this man who was her father, who shook her awake,
fondled her in the night, gave her chills and nightmares,
gainful reasons to kill all men she'd ever meet. Claire
held on with numbing force, her hand steady as sculpted
ice, my thumb stroking for her thaw. I'd kissed her cheek,
just once, and just that one time she smiled at me, leaned in and
kissed me back. I was here for the sake of appearances, she a
lesbian, happy and proud, but her people were not in the know.
Mist settled on my glasses, on the casket, on the grass. When
no one was looking, I looked behind our grim group,
over my glasses, at a woman by herself. She held one rose,
pale yellow, and a slightly torn umbrella, her lips mouthing
quiet questions I wanted so to hear, those lips such a vibrant
red. *Dust to dust* . . . I squeezed Claire's hand and motioned,
she squeezed me back with an affirmative shrug.
The minister preached the longest prayer known to man,
uplifting the man so tethered to his earthly descent. *Let us be
vigilant against our* own *sin and destruction* . . . And I wanted this
woman to toss her umbrella, dance with me once in the rain, Woman
X, Woman from Nowhere I Could See. *Amen. Now, go in peace* . . .
You never know. Claire hocked and spit, her mother aghast with teary,
zombie eyes, my gaze beyond our circus, watching the woman kneel down.

The San Francisco Sonnets

For Toni Danieele Clark
(born June 4, 1972, and missing March 16, 1990)

Toni was last seen leaving her cousin's home in Oakland, California. She was driving to her home in San Francisco, but the Chevrolet was found on the San Francisco Bay Bridge, disabled and unoccupied.

Toni was two months pregnant at the time of her disappearance and a student-athlete.

The Taker Returns from a Ten-Minute Break

I look inside my 3 x 3, wonder how I'll make it through
this shift, this week, the next eighteen years, poker faced
and hand extended, making change and giving thanks
for it. They tell me the bridge is the place to do hard
thinking about your life—nothing follows you home,
save the grime and the gridlock. And maybe that's all
we need from a living, something to pay the backed up
bills, make it from here to the next available exit. So sure,
I'm thinking about life and crazy choices all the time—
which lanes sedans choose most, where every buck I touch
has been, what fool will risk it all on a single unpaid toll.
Taillights. Headlights. High beams against the night's killer
fog. The crisscross pattern that's bound to make some kind
of sense—with this Chevy bearing down on me, or the next.

San Francisco Bridge Suicide Jumper
Considers Relativity

Yes, it's true: on my dive to the surface, I passed
an ageless blue sedan, the keys still in the ignition,
mortarboard tassel in sway above the dash, her
narrowed eyes fixed on something far beyond me.
Her look called me coward and whatever can be seen
as worse—for not stopping my descent to respond
to her need, for reading the last page first, then throwing
my flawed text away. But I get ahead of myself.
We all do. As if we are in a rush to do the damn thing,
get the living over with, move on to the juicier parts. No one
shares how, on the way down, you hear clarity in motion—
the traversable crevice that teaches the value of synapse. I know
that now and more—the single step we ought not to take,
the splash and swallow of all things swirling when we do.

The Missing Girl's Sister

Her room is still the same. It feels
like it's our second sun, time circling
this dark center, nothing altered
nearest this dense core. We wait.
I want to know my mother. I want
to feel her rage on me, see me trip
and fall. She tells me I am growing
up, and laminates my sister's absent life.
She sits inside, her eye on the phone,
hands smoothing bedspread folds,
timing dust dance by. My sister—so alive
in photographs with grainy eyes
of secrets. My mother says she hears
her voice. I tell her, *Yes, I know.*

Prom King Goes Stag His Senior Year

I'm thinking that they lied again, those people
who claim we all have that someone, one
woman for one man. And maybe it's some-
thing I did or not, but that special one never
crossed my path or ever passed a note my way.
Joey said I scared her off, being smart and debonair,
brainiac that I am. And Joey ought to know—
every month, a brand new babe, like a magnet
by his side. I want to be untouchable, the man
who calls the love shots out, then commits
to just one heart. Joey said, *Shoot for the king
and you're bound to find your queen*. So I tried.
And I won. But she's not here. And if she is,
she's changed her mind and doesn't want to say.

The Junior Detective's Wife Speaks Out
on the Day of Their Divorce

It wasn't only the strain of this case, how he'd come
home knotted, airborne, like a whip about to snap
over either side of my face, electrified and silent.
He believed she was alive somewhere, restless
and in struggle, in a place he couldn't locate but tried
to get to all the time. Especially at night. Oftentimes
in me. And he'd press on, keep digging long after
the brass turned his will to rust and our lives, too.
Dear God—I couldn't soothe the brittle, couldn't make
solid what time had turned to dust, his solo hunt a charged
metallic rain that stung and cut my ever-opened eyes.
That, and how he crushed the children's joy—those hugs
where they can't speak a word or ever take a needed breath.
He shattered glass, then swept it, then pushed us all away.

The Missing Girl's Mother

My life brims over with alternative endings.
So many words I should have spoken, fine
china I should have used. Tell me I should
have made her stay there the night, not try
to take that bridge. Maybe I was too strict.
Sometimes I pretend my daughter is away
—at some fancy school learning French,
in the Air Force, abroad, flying planes.
At work, I answer in questions. My world is
apostrophe on the way to contractions. At home,
I fly from the couch. They say they found her
keys, dangling. Maybe I was a good mother.
Tell me that I am a mother at all, my daughter
a rising of vapors. Explain to me, now, what I am.

Priest Refuses Comment
on Accident Driver's Acquittal

I find that most tend not to lie. No need—
we won't reveal a crime no matter what
the circumstance. I took my vows right out
of youth—too young to buy but not to pour.
And there were girls who gave me pause, made me
weigh my faith, this call to life, my choice.
My mother said we'd all be blessed. My dad
spit hard to pierce my side—meek son turned man,
now priest. Confessions make me cry each time.
I harbor sins, those bursts of red revealed.
To think that God absolves through man like me,
and I can order penance paid then move about
my day. (Your man was at the Stations twice,
alone each time, his body bowed in prayer.)

Olympic Hopeful Assesses Her Victory

So yeah, I trained like mad for this, giving up
the late night for the early morning rise.
Push-ups, suicides, weights in the gym,
a diet rich with green and snap. I'd stay
after practice to train on my own, tackle
the distance, take on the stairs long after
Coach blew the whistle and the team
called it quits. I thought it was the moon.
Thought it was that man up there, checking
out practice through chain link and trees,
but I know better now. It's just the wind
behind me, even when I am motionless,
gaining and pushing me aside. Yeah. Beside
and against me at the very same time.

The Missing Girl's Cousin

I hate the way they stare at me. Like just
because my ride was whack I have to bear
their disrespect. At holidays, they look at me,
the whole crew at the table, they glare and cut
their eyes away, like I don't ache like they do.
She was my bud, my hangout friend, she knew
'most all my secrets. Like the time when we cut
Chemistry . . . Now, see? I shouldn't tell that story.
They all think I made her do these crazy things
and it just wasn't like that. I taught her how
to breathe and run, to pace herself while sprinting,
to watch the movie play inside her head of how
she'd cross the finish. No, I gave that ride away
for free, would've paid some fool to take it.

The Present Song of Seagulls
on the San Francisco Bay

And even now we wait for her and cold—
the night a mess of mist, the human light
diffused and falling—on breaking crests,
on shadows trailing after. Every bridge
becomes the one she may have crossed
last and lost, each shore our angled next
new landing. No people ask what secret flights
we keep beneath our wings or ruffle us
to witness. Not our problem—we just soar
and catalogue: the crown of her head, his
uneven stupor, another night of watchfulness,
now you. No one looks for us in darkness. They
take us for granted, like light. *We know.* Listen.
And you thought this was our mating call. *We know.*

The Missing Girl's Boyfriend

I think I have a child somewhere. If he's
a boy, I'd call him Ted and name him
for my father. My dad was great and then
he died, hit twice by some drunk driver.
If she's a girl, her name's Lisette,
because I know she's pretty. I wonder
if she'd know my voice and understand
my absence. At night, I dream of baby
hands too slick to hold, while doors slam
in the distance. I filled my bedroom wall
with holes each time her mama called
my house. I'm learning there are layers to me,
like the layers to what I've lost. Maybe I'll
have other kids. First one, I'm naming Tony.

The Teacher Prepares
the Crisis Counseling Team

They try not to fall into the holes in the midst
of our classroom, the seat where he sat or the books
he once touched. And I do it, too—catch
myself taking breath before his surname
on the roll or blurting his first out of habit.
The rest of the day is a wash at those times,
the students and I lured too far into warp
and hypothetical to be any good for math or music.
In my desk is his folder: some pretests, origami,
my cryptic comments never shared, and more—
a folded note that says he likes that quiet girl,
still here. Today, in her seat in front of his,
she fidgets with her hair and face, pulls out
her own crisp ribbons, walks wide around his void.

Couple Tours Alcatraz
on Their Silver Anniversary

She says this to me, now—she's always wanted
a snapshot of me blank-faced behind bars, tiny
square of sunlight in the corner of the frame.
We stand in line to photograph what is
designed to be façade, each of us both
prisoner and voyeur, the captive spirit caught.
She says this, too—*Say gruel*—and I grip hard,
close my eyes to blinding flash. I can't find
whatever we lost on Treasure Island, the heart
that Tony Bennett swore would still be here.
Twenty-five years and here we are, casing a life,
avoiding the sad eyes of strangers. Off the boat,
now on shore, the tour guide slaps all us men
on our backs, then wishes us speedy parole.

The Missing Girl's Father

Day came when I had to quit my wife;
that meant walking away from our girls.
Their mother's all to blame, not me. She'd
flare up into mushroom clouds whenever
I got near them, singed my babies into silence.
I needed to be more than one line in her story.
Their mother spoiled them girls too much,
way too soft to do them any good. I caught
a train to Cleveland before they finished
elementary and never looked back once.
Not that I won't hurting, then, or even now.
I think I'm hurting more than her—my girls
swept back from me so many years before. Being
gone is being gone—no matter how you missing.

POLYGRAPH: THE GUILTY KNOWLEDGE TEST

• • •

No. The question was who is responsible for the suffering of your mother.

It is dawn on DeKalb and your mother comes home without breath
to scream, clearing a path to you with fingers splayed. You see trails
of her blood on the sidewalk behind her, branching lines of her blood
running down her weak legs, caked blood on her bare, uncut feet

and you breathe for her.

When you ask her who did this she says she can't say.
You pray for certain language, eyes to see around statues of saints.

What do you remember about the earth?

When they call off the rescue, you wonder whose voice
commands the divers to resurface, the lifeboats to return to shore, empty.

It is no one they show on the news. For the cameras,
they focus on sun-dazed bathers who underline the obvious, that it is late afternoon

on Coney Island's violent shore and Akira
is below and beyond. You, too, were in those waters, not that day but days before,

covered at once with a mosaic of fragments.
Yes, a tide that jostles stress from your bones, unearths grains beneath you,

then pushes you away like a gorgeous, well-spoiled lover.
Each time, you understand you could die like this, too convoluted to find your way

to air, the virulent waves close and in cahoots
to claim you. You bargain with the sea, inch deeper with each buckling crash.

How strong must you be to save yourself
from lure, to swim against natural, surrounded by your most abundant element?

What are the consequences of silence?

When it is late and you sit in the darkness,
safe in your easy chair at the far side
of your bedroom, you permit yourself
to think about the praying man in black.

You are trying to get home and there
he is, blocking your path, his palms
touching each other, his head bent
as in reverence, his thin lips mouthing

something you're not supposed to
hear. You are trying to get home
and this man is walking toward you,
and you are singing Chic or En Vogue

in the freeway's middle lane, your feeble
attempt to stay awake, and his eyes
are closed when you swerve around him,
shout obscenities at him, thick like exhaust.

And when you arrive at your door,
and your husband asks about your
drive, and your children hug your legs
and waist, you start to tell them about

the man who parked on the shoulder
then walked away from his car, tried
to make victims of you both. But life
intrudes—that tall stack of mail to open,

dishes awaiting their wash, a long list
of phone calls to return to your creditors.
And you *know* you swerved and missed
him. You know you safely made it home.

Tell me what you know about dismemberment

You knew you would feel something.

The new dentist comments on the depth of your roots,
their curvatures too pronounced to relieve you

of all your pain, but you guessed this early on,
when nothing could render you numb or detached.

There are holes where bone should be, vacancies
your tongue finds at random, learns to penetrate

like love. You survive the Massachusetts hills
through powdery snow that muffles your steps,

your voice distant through Darvon, your cotton-packed cheeks.
You say you love your father. You are the dentist's little girl.

You are Exhibit A in the spring dental journals, stepchild
of Clorets, that banned silver compound, a surface polish

on the go. Observe the chair-side fountain that gurgles
for your blood, the crumbling teeth you swallow like food,

the disintegrating jawbone when you chew the icy air.

Describe a morning you woke without fear

It is four in the darkness and you cannot breathe.
You cannot will your chest to expand, and suddenly,
this is all right. You grope for the language of internal
surrender. Every day, you have a choice, this choice.

Your left hand memorizes the grooves and nicks
in your mother's headboard. The textured flaws
keep you holding on and sane. You are used to living
on the memories of breath in your body, savoring

history. And so, your routine—two handfuls
of hospital visits each month—trips for breath in Brooklyn
when you are close to the unconscious edge. You race
for adrenaline to turn your heaves into tremors, to let

your fingers trace the oxygen that patterns your plastic tent.
And when you sleep, you are a fish, tired of her flop, too spent
to extract the valuable from the extraneous, another waterless day.
This day, your eyes focus on your mother's bedside table,

her only good watch, stopped. Your pale green canister of Isuprel,
empty for weeks—your Tedrol tablets, expired—your mind, alive
and dancing. When the voice of stars beckons, you follow, inside out.
You see your mouth. You touch your lungs. Your breath is incandescent.

And what would you say if you could?

When a boy presents you
with the bicycle of your dreams,
the one you described to him
the last time you met in front
of his mother's full house,
it means the boy loves you.

And even if you know
he's too young to have a job
and his family has no money
to spare, you know this is
his way of winning your favor,
his way of catching your eye.

And even though this bicycle
was once beneath a girl
like you, who loves the wind
and the rise of her streamers
when she pedals down hills,
he says it is yours now, he paid

for the privilege to give it to you.
And in another neighborhood,
miles from his, and yours,
there is a blood-stained girl
getting up from the ground,
one adult who lays lifeless,

another who will buy her
a replica, a speedy Schwinn
in pink and white, then question
the eyes of every black
male she ever encounters,
looking for reasons or guilt.

But all you see is the smile of the boy
who fidgets before you, who gives
what you said you wanted
more than life itself—those streamers,
that basket, the gleaming silver
bell he waits for you to ring.

How will you / have you prepare(d) for your death?

Most of what you consider involves the shift
of paper—the move of one tall stack over here

to several small piles over there. You think
of possessions—if anyone would like your china,

care to carry the dusty bowl your mother carted
away from her marriage. And the wood in your life,

the headboard you stained in the deepest of browns,
the pressboard chest of drawers that holds your gowns

and slips, the tables that graced your grandmother's
front parlor and knew the heavy weight of lace.

What will become of your diamonds? The rings
from your fingers that meant promise or survival,

your mother's final gift? Who will claim your yarn
of half-done projects, the skinny scarves, the cross-stitch

you dare not throw away? You think, too, of words,
the archiving of papers and the cataloguing of books,

but even this is not your work to do. There is someone
ready with strong, cupped hands, who knows the scent

of your skin in your absence, who is with you
in spite of the geography of the world. You will need

to do the hard work of permission. You, too, will need
to stand before the threshold and ask if you may cross.

NOTE

The title questions posed in the sections "Polygraph: The Control Questions" and "Polygraph: The Guilty Knowledge Test" are titles of poems from Bhanu Kapil Rider's *The Vertical Interrogation of Strangers* (Kelsey St. Press, 2001). While Rider posed her questions to women of Indian descent to find a way to freedom and peace, I believe these questions should be answered in truth by every woman at least once during the course of her life.

THE FELIX POLLAK PRIZE IN POETRY
Ronald Wallace, General Editor

Now We're Getting Somewhere • David Clewell
   Henry Taylor, Judge, 1994

The Legend of Light • Bob Hicok
   Carolyn Kizer, Judge, 1995

Fragments in Us: Recent and Earlier Poems • Dennis Trudell
   Philip Levine, Judge, 1996

Don't Explain • Betsy Sholl
   Rita Dove, Judge, 1997

Mrs. Dumpty • Chana Bloch
   Donald Hall, Judge, 1998

Liver • Charles Harper Webb
   Robert Bly, Judge, 1999

Ejo: Poems, Rwanda, 1991–1994 • Derick Burleson
   Alicia Ostriker, Judge, 2000

Borrowed Dress • Cathy Colman
Mark Doty, Judge, 2001

Ripe • Roy Jacobstein
   Edward Hirsch, Judge, 2002

The Year We Studied Women • Bruce Snider
   Kelly Cherry, Judge, 2003

A Sail to Great Island • Alan Feldman
   Carl Dennis, Judge, 2004

Funny • Jennifer Michael Hecht
   Billy Collins, Judge, 2005

Reunion • Fleda Brown
   Linda Gregerson, Judge, 2007

The Royal Baker's Daughter • Barbara Goldberg
    David St. John, Judge, 2008

Falling Brick Kills Local Man • Mark Kraushaar
    Marilyn Nelson, Judge, 2009

The Lightning That Strikes the Neighbors' House • Nick Lantz
    Robert Pinsky, Judge, 2010

Last Seen • Jacqueline Jones LaMon
    Cornelius Eady, Judge, 2011